Dressing Up

D1695138

Cockleshell Bay is a town near the sea,
With seagulls and sunshine and sand.
There are shops that sell ices and bright-coloured kites
That fly from a string in your hand.
There are white-painted houses along the sea front,
And one's called 'The Bucket and Spade'.
It's where people stay, and two children play,
With all the good friends that they've made.
So meet – Robin and Rosie of Cockleshell Bay.

Story by Brian Trueman
from the Cosgrove Hall series

Characters designed by Bridget Appleby
Backgrounds drawn by Avril Turner

Robin and Rosie were in the kitchen. They'd finished
their breakfast and put all the plates and things
in the sink to be washed.
"Let's go and see if Mr Ship is in his yard," said Rosie.

"Yes, let's," said Robin, "but we'd better tell
Mum first. She's upstairs."
But before he left, Mrs Cockle came in.
"Mum," started Robin, "we're going to . . ."
"Not now," interrupted Mrs Cockle. "I'm busy."

She looked in a cupboard. "Now *where* did I put those dusters?" she said, trying one cupboard after another. "Ah! Here they are!" And she hurried out.

"We'd better tell someone else then," said Robin.
Just then, Mr Cockle came in, in even more
of a hurry than *Mrs* Cockle.
He was shouting, "Helen! Where did you say?"
"Dad . . ." said Rosie . . .
"Not now, Rosie. I've lost some drawings."
He couldn't find them, and went out, muttering.

"Well," said Rosie, a bit cross. "How can we tell people where we're going if they won't stand still to listen."
"Finished breakfast, my dears?" said Gran Routy, coming in.
"Yes," said Rosie, "and we've been trying to tell Mum . . ."
"Trying's the word," said Gran Routy.

"You won't get anyone to listen to your stories today.
We're spring cleaning. Where did I put the stuff
for cleaning the bath?"
"But Gran . . ." said Robin.
"No 'Buts'. We're too busy today. I'd go and see
if Mr Ship's in his yard."
"But, Gran, that's . . ." began Robin, but Gran Routy had gone.

Robin and Rosie crossed their back garden to the boatyard. "Mr Ship!" they called. A muffled reply came back, as they reached the steps which led up to his house above the shed. "I'm in my house."

Robin looked about him. "Gosh! I think there must have
been an earthquake."
"Why?" asked Rosie, "what's the . . . Gosh! Yes!"

They peered under things and around things.
Everything was spread about higgledy piggledy.
There were boxes, sacks, bits of cloth and carpet,
pictures, books, paint brushes, tools . . .

"Hello Mr Ship! Are you all right? What happened?"
Mr Ship looked surprised. "All right? Why?"
"Have you been burgled?" said Rosie,
"or was it a storm?" "Bless me no! I'm just
spring cleaning."

Robin and Rosie looked at each other. "Oh no!"
They explained to Mr Ship that all the adults
in the Bucket and Spade were spring cleaning too,
and were much too busy to talk to them.

Mr Ship agreed. "'Taint a very nice job, but it's got
to be done. All I do is find lots of rubbish,
but nothing I want to throw away!"
Rosie spotted something. "Ooh!" she squeaked,
"What a lovely box!"

"That's my old sea chest," said Mr Ship. "You might find
one or two bits and pieces in there."
"Ooh! Can we look?"
"'Course," said Mr Ship, sitting down to drink his tea.
Robin opened the lid. "Ooh! Clothes!"

"No. Uniforms. That's my old sea-going kit," said Mr Ship.
"Can we try it on?"
"Yes. May be a bit big for you, though."

When they were dressed, they did look *very* funny,
because all the clothes were much too big for them.
"I keep treading on the bottoms of the trousers," said
Robin, "and . . ."
". . . falling over," said Rosie, as Robin tripped.

Rosie laughed so much that her hat fell right
over her eyes. "Ooh! I can't see where I'm going!"
"Look out!" shouted Robin. "You're heading straight for the . . ."
"Whoops!" shouted Rosie. She tumbled head-first
into the sea chest.

Robin laughed so much that he couldn't get up, and Mr Ship
gulped some tea down the wrong way, and laughed and coughed
all at the same time, and *he* couldn't get up either.
And Rosie kept shouting for someone to help her out.

When they'd stopped laughing, Robin and Mr Ship took a leg
each and pulled. "We'll do it sailor-fashion," said Mr Ship,
and he began to sing:
"It's anchors aweigh; we're sailing today;
so heave on the anchor chain, boys!"

"For though you may roam, it's a joy to be home,
and we'll soon be in port again, boys!"

And they pulled, and Rosie was upright again.
"Phew!" she said. "It's dusty in there. It needs
spring cleaning."
"Mr Ship," said Robin, taking his jacket off. "What was that
song you were singing?"
"A sea shanty. You sing it when you're hauling on ropes."
"Is there any more?"

"Well . . . We sail to the East, we sail to the West,
We sail to the Spanish Main.
Then it's 'Anchors aweigh'
Back to Cockleshell Bay,
For that's where a sailor's heart is."
"Ooh! Smashing," cried Robin and Rosie. "Sing it again!"

But before they could, Gran Routy called.
It was lunchtime. So Robin and Rosie went back
to 'The Bucket and Spade' Guest House.

Mr and Mrs Cockle and Gran Routy were looking for a duster,
some drawings, and the stuff to clean the sink with.
Can you help to find them?

This Thames Magnet edition first published in Great Britain 1985
by Methuen Children's Books Ltd
11 New Fetter Lane, London EC4P 4EE
in association with Thames Television International Ltd
149 Tottenham Court Road, London W1P 9LL
Copyright © 1982 Cosgrove Hall Productions Ltd
Printed in Great Britain
ISBN 0 423 01550X
Cockleshell Bay is a Cosgrove Hall Productions film series
The Cockleshell Bay stories were first produced
as single short stories by Marks and Spencer p.l.c.